KT-148-084

STAR WARS™

I AM
YOUR
FATHER

Written by Amy Richau and Dan Zehr

Contents

Introduction

Every child and Padawan learner is different.
But many of the most influential lessons a parent,
mentor, guardian, or teacher can impart are
the same no matter what star system you come
from. Allow this book to help you on your path.
Beru Lars, Iden Versio, and Bail Organa will inspire
you to support your own hero. Kanan Jarrus,
Leia Organa, and Qui-Gon Jinn will remind
you that the hard work of providing guidance
can have an immeasurable impact on both
your youngling and the rest of the galaxy.

These roles are never easy. Your apprentice
is bound to stray at times or challenge your views.
But the frustrations are repaid tenfold when
those you care for set out by themselves.
Let *Star Wars: I Am Your Father* help you in your
journey as a caregiver to instil empathy,
knowledge, persistence, and courage
in the young person you care about.

Mentoring

"WE HAVE HOPE. HOPE THAT THINGS WILL GET BETTER. AND THEY WILL."

Hera to the *Ghost*'s crew
STAR WARS REBELS

Mentoring

Stand up for what's right

Rebel leader Hera Syndulla stands out for her belief in a future free from tyranny and her steadfast determination to achieve it. She refuses to give up on this dream and fights the evil Empire in any way she can, leading a rebel assault to liberate the planet Lothal. Hera keeps her crew on the *Ghost* focused by offering them hope. Advocate for a better tomorrow through your actions and your words, and those who look up to you might just pick up the cause as well.

"NO. I AM YOUR FATHER!"

Darth Vader to Luke Skywalker
THE EMPIRE STRIKES BACK

Mentoring

Be honest

When Darth Vader reveals that he is Luke Skywalker's father, Luke finds the information hard to hear. Some truths can expose painful memories or conflict with another person's point of view. It can be scary to reveal a secret you think others may judge you for, but deceiving those you love the most can lead to the dark side. Being candid and facing difficult conversations head-on will make it easier for those you care for to emulate this behaviour and will strengthen your relationships in the long run.

"Why should I help anybody? I got no one."
– BOBA FETT

"It is the honourable thing to do. It's what your father would have wanted."
– HONDO OHNAKA

Boba Fett and Hondo Ohnaka
STAR WARS: THE CLONE WARS

Mentoring

Offer a better choice

Wise words can come from anyone, even
a dashing space pirate like Hondo Ohnaka. The
young Boba Fett has a choice to make: save lives
by informing a Jedi of their location, or let them
perish. Boba is still furious over his father's death
at the hands of a Jedi, but Hondo helps him by
reminding him what Boba's father would have
wanted. If you see someone struggling with
a moral dilemma, remind them of the bigger
picture and the consequences of their choices.
While it is still their decision to make, another
perspective might help them pick the right path.

"In my experience, when you think you understand the Force, you realize just how little you know."

Ahsoka Tano to Ezra Bridger
STAR WARS REBELS

Mentoring

Engender curiosity

Ahsoka Tano is a powerful and experienced Force user. When she shares with Ezra Bridger how little she knows about the Force, the young Jedi-in-training cannot help but be intrigued. Ahsoka's fascination with the mystical energy field serves as a catalyst for Ezra to further his studies. By continuing to grow in our own understanding, we can inspire those we care for to realize that there is always more to learn. It's a big galaxy after all.

"THIS IS THE WAY."

The Armorer
THE MANDALORIAN

Mentoring

Set an example

The Armorer is a pillar of her Mandalorian community who follows a set of beliefs known as the Way. Her people's survival depends on them observing these principles and supporting each other. If you're leading a team, whether it is in sports, at work, or a group of Mandalorian warriors, uphold the rules in a fair and measured way. By keeping a cool head and focusing on the broader view, you'll inspire those who follow you to do the same.

Encouragement

"You lost.
But you lost well."

Jarek Yeager to Kazuda Xiono
STAR WARS RESISTANCE

Find the positive

The best mentors and caregivers find lessons in both successes and defeats. Hotshot pilot Kazuda Xiono doesn't listen to starfighter veteran Jarek Yeager's warnings about pushing his ship too far in his first race. But rather than admonish him, Yeager chooses to focus on Kaz's impressive piloting skills that allowed him to escape a dangerous situation. It's never a good idea to kick someone when they are down. As wise Jedi Master Yoda once said, "The greatest teacher, failure is."

"Now be brave, and don't look back."

Shmi Skywalker to Anakin Skywalker
THE PHANTOM MENACE

Seize the opportunity

When Shmi Skywalker's son, Anakin, is offered an opportunity to fulfil his dream and become a Jedi Knight, she knows that he has to take it. Shmi encourages him, even though she does not want them to be separated. Encourage those you care for to pursue difficult, yet rewarding, opportunities. Providing support for those who look up to you can help alleviate some of the anxiety involved in taking on a big challenge and help them gain the confidence they need to move forwards.

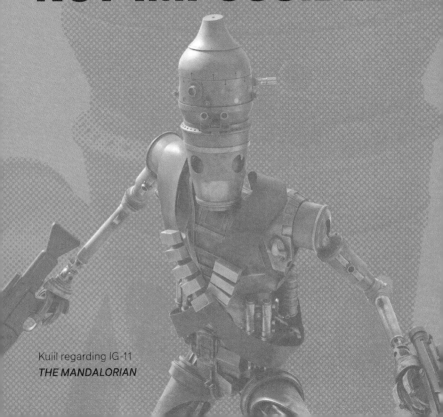

"RECONSTRUCTION WAS QUITE DIFFICULT. BUT, NOT IMPOSSIBLE."

Kuiil regarding IG-11
THE MANDALORIAN

Give them time

The Ugnaught Kuiil has a daunting task ahead of him – helping the droid IG-11 transform himself from a ruthless killing machine into a nurturing caregiver. Kuiil starts small, by demonstrating the kind behaviour he wants the droid to exhibit and praising IG-11 when he mimics his actions. Whether you are trying to encourage someone in your team to work smarter or you are dealing with an emotional outburst from a child, being patient and showing compassion can encourage the behaviour you desire. Remember, while it's rarely easy or quick, change is always possible. IG-11 would now rather help people than dole out death and destruction.

"It means so much to him."

Beru Lars regarding Luke Skywalker
A NEW HOPE

Show interest

Those we care for may have aspirations that differ from our own ideas for them, nevertheless their dreams are worthy of further exploration. Luke Skywalker doesn't want to be a moisture farmer like his aunt and uncle. He longs to leave the dusty landscape of Tatooine and forge his own path. Beru believes in him and wants him to pursue his goals. Encourage and support your young person's choices and reinforce their self-confidence as they start to explore their talents and gifts.

"WE FIGHT SO OTHERS CAN LIVE."

Iden Versio to Zay Versio
STAR WARS: BATTLEFRONT II

Encouragement

Share your motivations

Rebellions are built on hope. Belief, whether it comes with large or small sacrifices, matters when you're fighting for something you hold dear. Iden Versio leaves the Empire to join the Rebel Alliance and later fights the First Order alongside her daughter, Zay. In her final moments, Iden reminds Zay how much she means to her and divulges how their mission could benefit others. Explain why your passions are meaningful to you and how they can also change the world (or the galaxy). Those you care for may continue your legacy or find their own cause to support.

Lessons Learnt

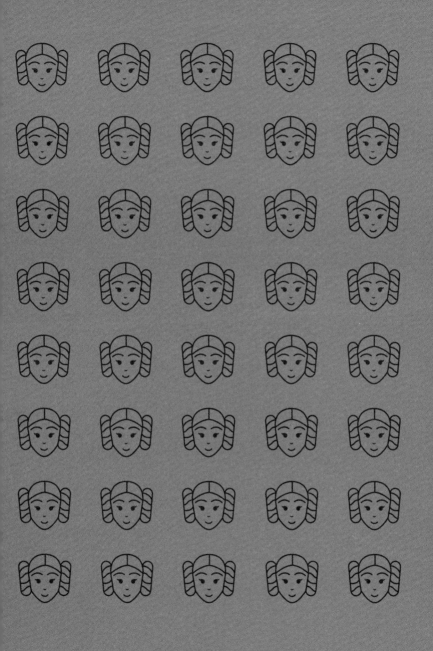

"WE TOOK DOWN A DREADNOUGHT."

– POE

"AT WHAT COST?"

– LEIA

Poe Dameron and Leia Organa
THE LAST JEDI

Impart responsibility

General Organa needs to raise a new generation of leaders, including Commander Poe Dameron. She entrusts him with the lives of their pilots and is not pleased when he acts in a reckless manner to destroy an enemy ship. Poe's ego stops him from taking ownership of the cost, so Leia demotes him to force him to reconsider his outlook. It might take tough love to help someone look at things through a different lens, but another perspective can help those you care for to take responsibility for their choices.

"Keep your concentration here and now, where it belongs."

Qui-Gon Jinn to Obi-Wan Kenobi
THE PHANTOM MENACE

Keep them focused

Jedi Master Qui-Gon Jinn is one of the Order's finest teachers. On a mission, his Padawan Obi-Wan Kenobi is concerned about a distant threat he senses, but Qui-Gon is quick to reorient his Padawan's attention to ensure their success in what they're doing right now. Don't be afraid to be forthright with those around you. There's a time for praise and a time for critique in a relationship between a young person and someone they look up to. If you see your Padawan drifting away from what they should be focusing on, take a moment to set their concentration back on track.

"If you choose to face Vader, you will do it alone. I cannot interfere."

Obi-Wan Kenobi to Luke Skywalker
THE EMPIRE STRIKES BACK

Set boundaries

It's natural for caregivers to be tempted to swoop in and save the day when their younglings are in trouble, such as struggling with a difficult piece of homework. But it's not always the right call – for the young person or the adult who looks after them. Interfering may result in a swift victory but can hinder long-term growth. Obi-Wan Kenobi knew as much when he told Luke Skywalker he could not help him if he chose to leave his training unfinished and face Darth Vader. Know when it is time for your apprentice to go it alone. Young people are bound to make decisions their caregivers do not approve of, but it's their life and they must make their own choices.

"DO. OR DO NOT. THERE IS NO TRY."

Yoda to Luke Skywalker
THE EMPIRE STRIKES BACK

Give your best to be your best

Luke Skywalker becomes impatient and exhausted during his Jedi training with Yoda. However, the 900-year-old Jedi Master is not interested in lacklustre effort! He knows that Luke is giving excuses and not giving his all. We prefer our Padawans to work hard, but don't be surprised when, at times, that doesn't happen. Take a moment to understand their reluctance and redirect them so they can give their best. If they want to be the best Jedi they can be, tell them that they have to put in the time.

"Slow down. The Force is trying to tell you something. Listen to it."

Kanan Jarrus to Ezra Bridger
STAR WARS REBELS

Be patient

Jedi Knight Kanan Jarrus teaches his Padawan, Ezra Bridger, one of life's most difficult lessons: patience. Ezra's enthusiasm often gets the better of him, which reinforces his mentor's quiet resolve that he shouldn't give Ezra all of the answers. When someone in your care is impatient, perhaps that is the best time to encourage them to step back. They need to take a deep breath and appreciate it is the journey, not the destination, that helps us learn life's most valuable lessons.

Trust

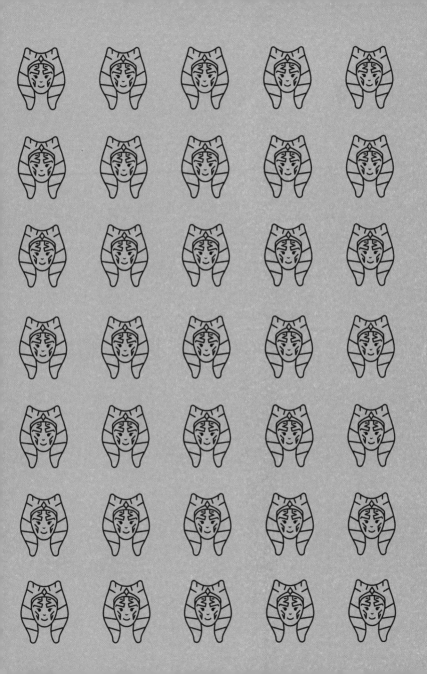

"Never be afraid of who you are."

Leia Organa to Rey
THE RISE OF SKYWALKER

Trust

Promote self-belief

General Leia Organa passes on perhaps her most personal advice to her Padawan Rey when she tells her not to hide from who she is. Leia knows this better than anyone in the galaxy because she was publicly revealed as the daughter of the evil Sith Lord, Darth Vader! When you believe in yourself – your true self – no matter what others think, you provide a powerful example to all.

"I WOULD TRUST HER WITH MY LIFE."

Bail Organa regarding Leia Organa
ROGUE ONE: A STAR WARS STORY

Trust

Support your own hero

Bail Organa is one of the founders of the Rebel Alliance against the Galactic Empire. He also raised one of its greatest leaders, Leia Organa. When the Rebellion is at its most desperate hour, Bail immediately entrusts his daughter, Leia, with a dangerous and vital mission. The skills that you have picked up in order to succeed in uncertain times provide valuable information. Share what you have learnt, big or small. Your protégés will build on this knowledge and continue to thrive, even when you are gone.

"I was a foundling."

Din Djarin to Grogu
THE MANDALORIAN

Trust

Find common ground

The biggest surprises can come in the smallest of packages. Bounty hunter Din Djarin (Mando) lives by the code of his trade and the traditions of his fellow Mandalorians until a small child named Grogu unexpectedly comes into his life. Rescued by a Mandalorian himself during his childhood, Djarin is touched by the youngling's plight so decides to start protecting him. Like Mando, you might often think of yourself as a loner. Take the time to find shared experiences, interests, or traits that you can build upon. Maybe your paths were meant to cross.

"FEEL. DON'T THINK. USE YOUR INSTINCTS."

Qui-Gon Jinn to Anakin Skywalker
THE PHANTOM MENACE

Trust

Help them overcome self-doubts

Jedi Master Qui-Gon Jinn wisely instructs
the young and powerful Force-user Anakin
Skywalker to concentrate on the moment and
not overthink during a dangerous podrace.
Qui-Gon's calm words empower Anakin to trust
in himself. Whether it be nerves before an exam
or a new situation, teach those in your care to set
aside their negative thoughts and trust that they
already possess what is required to succeed.

"SHE'S TRYING TO SAVE HER FAMILY, HUNTER. I'D DO THE SAME FOR YOU."

Omega to Hunter
STAR WARS: THE BAD BATCH

Trust

Listen to children

When you are an adult, it can be tempting
to dismiss the opinions of children. The clone
mercenary Hunter ignores a plea for help, as he
is wary of the risks. However, his charge Omega
wants to offer aid and pushes back, letting him
know that she has a different idea of what the
right action is for the situation. Even though
adults may think they know best, it isn't always
the case. Don't dismiss a child's point of view just
because you are older. Kids might see the world
from a different perspective and could offer
valuable insight that you haven't considered.

Acceptance

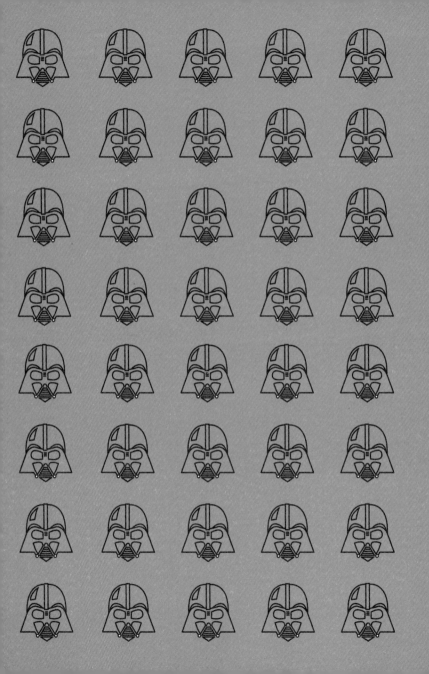

"I'M SORRY."
– LUKE

"I KNOW."
– LEIA

Luke Skywalker and Leia Organa
THE LAST JEDI

No one has all the answers

During the Battle of Crait, Luke and Leia share
a sorrowful moment over the actions of Leia's
son, the villain Kylo Ren. Every caregiver has
times when they are certain they have let down
their youngling in some way. Regret or guilt from
past actions can be quite painful, especially if
those they care for have taken a different path.
Accept that relationships may have moments
of difficulty and hold out hope that you'll find
a way back to one another someday.

"THIS IS WHERE I'M SUPPOSED TO BE. YOU'RE MY FAMILY."

Ezra to the crew of the *Ghost*
STAR WARS REBELS

Find your place

Ezra Bridger's mum and dad disappeared when he was seven years old, so he spent much of his life without his family, trying to find his place. When he meets the crew of the *Ghost*, he discovers a ragtag bunch of misfits who accept him, support him, and become his family. Find where you belong and others you can connect with. While it might take time and effort, these individuals can become members of your family and offer support in a sometimes scary galaxy.

"I HAVE TO FACE HIM."

Luke Skywalker to Leia Organa
RETURN OF THE JEDI

Acceptance

Running away won't solve your problems

After Luke Skywalker reveals to Leia Organa that Darth Vader is their father and that he plans to face him, Leia initially expresses reservations about Luke's objective. Sometimes acknowledging and discussing a disagreement is the best way to resolve it. Support those you care for as they process difficult news and be understanding that everyone handles conflicts differently.

"That might be the Mandalorian way, but it's not my way."

Sabine Wren to Ursa Wren
STAR WARS REBELS

Acceptance

See young people for who they are

Every child rebels in some way. Ursa Wren is hesitant to welcome back her daughter, Sabine, into their Mandalorian clan after she left and joined the Rebellion. But Ursa takes the time to listen to her daughter and see her for the leader she has become. Those you care for may make choices that don't make sense to you, but they are still an important part of your life. See the young person for who they truly are, not through the lens of who you wanted them to be.

"I've accepted the truth that you were once Anakin Skywalker, my father."

Luke Skywalker to Darth Vader
RETURN OF THE JEDI

You can't change your family's past

On the Forest Moon of Endor, Luke Skywalker reveals that he knows and accepts the truth of his father's history. Time has passed since their duel on Cloud City, when Vader's shocking revelation greatly upset Luke. The young Jedi has since come to terms with his father's identity. While no one can change the past, it's never too late for your own actions to make a positive difference in the galaxy.

Project Editor Matt Jones
Project Art Editor Stefan Georgiou
Production Editor Marc Staples
Senior Producer Mary Slater
Managing Editor Emma Grange
Managing Art Editor Vicky Short
Publishing Director Mark Searle

Book concept by Beth Davies

DK would like to thank: Brett Rector, Michael Siglain, Troy Alders, Kelsey Sharpe, Kate Izquierdo, Sarah Williams, Jackey Cabrera, Elinor De La Torre, and Shahana Alam at Lucasfilm; Chelsea Alon at Disney Publishing; Pamela Afram for editorial assistance; Chris Gould for design assistance; Julia March for proofreading and Anglicization; Jennette ElNaggar for proofreading and Americanization; and Heidi Dorr for authenticity reading.

First published in Great Britain in 2022 by
Dorling Kindersley Limited
DK, One Embassy Gardens, 8 Viaduct Gardens,
London, SW11 7BW

The authorised representative in the EEA is
Dorling Kindersley Verlag GmbH. Arnulfstr. 124,
80636 Munich, Germany

Page design copyright © 2022 Dorling Kindersley Limited
A Penguin Random House Company
10 9 8 7 6 5 4 3 2 1
001–327884–May/2022

© & TM 2022 LUCASFILM LTD.

A CIP catalogue record for this book
is available from the British Library.
ISBN: 978-0-24154-849-3

Printed and bound in China

For the curious

www.dk.com

www.starwars.com

MIX
Paper from
responsible sources
FSC™ C018179

This book was made with Forest Stewardship Council ™ certified paper – one small step in DK's commitment to a sustainable future. For more information go to www.dk.com/our-green-pledge